HOW TO BLEND FAMILIES

A Guide for Step Parents

Blending Families after Divorce and Remarriage

by Debra Chapoton B.A., M.A.T. Oakland University

and

Paul Chapoton B.A., M.A.in Guidance & Counseling, Oakland University, Ed. Spec. Wayne State University

ISBN: 9781792784675

Introduction: Who We Are

Debra and Paul Chapoton

Parents of a Blended Family

When Paul and I married our children were 6, 8, 10, and 11. My girls were 8 and 11 and his daughter was 10 and his son was 6. We both had full custody. Divorce and remarriage was challenging for all of us, but we succeeded as a family and all of the kids have grown into wonderful, productive adults with children of their own.

We've been in your shoes. Divorce is awful. Between us we had five college degrees and thought we could figure everything out easy as pie. But we still had a rough time blending our families. Now, with over half a century (combined) of teaching behind us and many years of co-parenting we've written this guide to help others who, for whatever sad reason, find themselves trying to blend two distinct — and probably hurting—families. Paul has been a teacher, coach, and a personal life counselor. I have been a teacher as well as a published author of educational materials, fiction, and non-fiction. I've been published in multiple countries and three languages. Here's what we learned from our experience.

TABLE OF CONTENTS

Chapter One: Start Fresh

Get a New Place

This may be really hard, especially with the real estate market the way it is, but everyone needs to feel that the house is theirs--their HOME. Otherwise, somebody is going to feel like a visitor, somebody is going to feel intruded upon, somebody is going to be resentful, somebody is going to feel like an outsider and your family will have difficulty blending.

If one of you already has a home big enough to accommodate your new spouse and step-kids, DO NOT consider it. For the reasons stated above this is a bad idea. The only exception is if it's for a short time--measured in weeks--while you're buying or building a bigger place.

Dos and Don'ts

Do put locks on their doors. They're in a new situation and need to feel some control as well as the right to privacy and space.

Do set boundaries. Everyone should remember to knock on closed doors and announce themselves at open doors. It's good training for the future as well as the current transition period.

Do try to have a bedroom for each child. If two of the same sex kids shared a room before, it would be all right to continue that, but if a child has to suddenly share a room there will be problems.

Don't make new step-siblings share a room.

Don't have siblings of the opposite sex share a room. If that means you need a five bedroom house then either stretch the budget or change the neighborhood. The health of your new family is more important.

True story—names changed:

Jim, a teacher, and Diane got married in the summer when their four kids, two each, were out of school. Jim moved into Diane's house and because he had the summer off he drove a half an hour back to his ex-wife's house every morning to pick up his kids and bring them to Diane's for the day. They had no rooms to stay in while they visited and, for sure, those kids felt like visitors. They had to make the trip back to their old home each night.

When school started the situation worsened. But Diane sold her house and the new family moved into a five bedroom house in Jim's kids' school district. Each child had their own room then. The family was able to blend, become friends, and a routine without a lot of travel smoothed things out a lot.

New Home Worksheet:

1) What are the minimum and maximum number of bedrooms you need?

_____ to _____

2) Who can share a bedroom?

_____ and _____

3) What are the minimum and maximum number of bathrooms you need?

_____ to _____

4) Who can share a bathroom?

_____

5) What schools do you want to be near?

_____

6) How close to work do you need to be?

_____

7) What other things do you need to consider?

_____

_____

_____

_____

Chapter Two: Start Talking

Get Counseling

Many insurance companies pay for this as long as there is a certified psychologist on staff at the counseling center you choose. It might be once a week for a few months or once a month for a year, but it will be vital for a good, strong start to blending your families and learning about one another.

Blended families will have issues to resolve. Sessions may include all members at first and subsequently allow for separate sessions with each child and/or the parents. Each family member's role is different and will have changed due to the new makeup of the family. A first born child may now be the middle child or the baby of the family may suddenly lose that spot to a new younger step-sister or -brother.

Patterns of interaction will strain at times, not to mention the obvious problem of confusion or maybe grief over the change in family structure.

Counseling is also helpful in identifying problems that may arise in the future based on the ages of each child. Dealing with preadolescents or teenagers is vastly different that bonding with babies and toddlers. There also may be attachment problems, relationship suspicions, or trust and resentment issues. Rivalries may emerge. Having regular sessions with a professional will ease the process.

Dos and Don'ts

Do expect depression, acting out, resentments, and mouthing off.

Do try to be compassionate, understanding, and patient.

Do react to immediate behavior problems, but don't punish or discipline your step-children (yet). (See chapter on Discipline)

Do begin counseling and/or therapy within weeks of blending families. The long term benefits far outweigh any short term inconvenience.

Don't limit the talking to the professional setting. Talk at the dinner table, in the car, while watching TV or playing games (yes, play games with kids!).

True story—names changed:

Laurie and Doug's marriage included her two daughters and his two ADD kids. It didn't help that Doug's ex-wife was the least maternal woman in the world or that Laurie's ex demanded unreasonable access to his kids, phoning them after bedtime or returning them from visitation quite late.

Professional counseling included individual sessions with the children where they were encouraged in "play therapy" to act out situations from home. Then later, with the counselor's insight, Laurie was able to learn how to deal with Doug's children's ADD problems and Doug found out why Laurie's girls were having such a hard time accepting him (their father threatened to withhold his love if they liked Doug).

Counseling Worksheet

1) Top 3 recommendations, name & phone:

_____

_____

_____

2) Best days and times for family appointments:

_____

_____

_____

3) Top concerns to discuss with counselor:

_____

_____

_____

_____

_____

_____ — _____

_____

_____

_____

Chapter Three: Start Scheduling

Visitations

Schedule visitations so that the family is all together or all away on the same weekends. Make sure pick-up and drop-off times are clearly understood by all parties. Does a weekend visitation start on Friday night or Saturday morning? What time, exactly? Discuss specifics with your ex. Do not negotiate through the kids.

Get a physical calendar and put it where everyone can see it. Clearly mark weekends and weeknights when kids are away as well as the many daily and weekly events that will crowd your life: dentist appointments, band practice, volleyball, confirmation class, sleepovers, etc. Save the calendars. You'll be amazed some day at how you got through the busiest time of your life.

With four kids in various activities inside and outside of school there were weeks when we had upwards of thirty things going on (and I have the calendar to prove it—the record was 56).

Trust me, keeping the ex-spouse's visitation (or your visitation) on coordinated weekends will make blending your families so much easier. Kids don't want to miss anything or find out that you took the step-kids shopping while they were away. If half of your new family is off with the other parent you aren't blending, you're separating.

The added advantage is that now you and your new spouse have some alone time together to keep the new marriage strong.

Dos and Don'ts

Do manage a calendar.

Don't separate the new family into different weekends.

Don't negotiate visitation through the kids. Talk directly to your ex. (It may be emotional, but it's better to rile up your emotions rather than the kids'.)

True story—names changed:

Darla and Pierre's attempt at blending their family was going pretty well until Darla's twelve year old daughter, Stephanie, needed to attend Wednesday night confirmation class at their church. This was an eight week course with make-up classes on the weekends.

Stephanie's real father had Wednesday night visitation, but rather than switch to a different night for a couple of months he refused. He would not take her to attend her class because it was "his visitation time" as decreed in the court order. The same thing happened for the make-up classes that fell on his weekends; he wouldn't give up an hour of "his time" for her to attend.

Eventually she did complete her requirements, but the confusion, frustration, and anger left scars.

Don't be that parent. Be flexible.

Calendar Worksheet:

Kids' weekends home:

_____

Kids' weekends away:

_____

Kids' weeknight visitation:

_____

Sports practices by day and time (and kid):

_____

_____

_____

_____

_____

Other regularly scheduled activities:

_____

_____

_____

Occasional add ons:

_____

Chapter Four: Start Traditions

Get Creative

You probably had some traditions in your "previous life." Family traditions range from daily routines like a story before bedtime to weekly things like game night and yearly ones like a first day of school photo. Keep doing those personal things that exist between you and your child and, if possible, bring the new members into the activities that will promote family togetherness.

Get creative. Discuss with your new spouse what things you could invent to make everyone feel like a special member of this new unit. Here are some ideas:

Pick a new vacation spot. If you and your ex always took the kids to the same beach resort don't go back with the new family. Leave those memories intact for your child. They will be precious to him or her. Your new family can enjoy fresh memories at a different resort.

Have a movie night. Sometimes just being all together with no other pressure to get along is the best thing especially if the kids are older and resisting the blend. Be ready to express your opinion of the movie and then ask them questions about what they thought.

Make up a family holiday, name it, and create activities to associate with it. For example, if your exes have the kids for Thanksgiving then make Friday "Steaksgiving" and grill sirloins outside or take them to a steakhouse restaurant. Afterwards go bowling or have a Monopoly showdown.

Have a family board game night. This is great way to get everyone to know one another. There are several board games that are available which have this as their underlying goal. An Internet search will give you many suggestions. Or, play the games that each kid already enjoys. This is also a great time to teach about sportsmanship and how to be a good winner and a good loser.

Plan on making Christmas (Thanksgiving, Easter, the 4th of July) a different day in your house. (We started having Christmas on the weekend before – everybody knew the schedule and it didn't conflict with step-families or ex-spouses and it took the anxiety away from coordinating pick-ups and drop-offs on Christmas Eve or Christmas morning. The tradition has continued and has withstood the pressures of extended families, in-laws, and multiple grandparents now that the kids are married.)

Go to church together. Hopefully you and your new spouse have already talked about this and have the same views on religion, which will make things a whole lot easier, tough as they are. The last thing you want to do is go in different directions on Sundays and split your new family. If it means leaving your former church and joining a new church together then do it. If your ex doesn't take them to church or takes them somewhere else on weekends they're not with you, that's fine. Let your kids get the solid foundation on the Sundays they're with you. Enjoy the blessings.

Dos and Don'ts

Don't try to outdo your ex on vacation plans. Keep things simple and stress free.

Do discuss the details of the new traditions with your kids.

Don't criticize anyone's opinions or their feelings.

Don't interfere with your ex's traditions.

True story—names changed:

Elizabeth and Keith took their blended family, including Nikki, Brad, Erika, and Ashley, to a vacation home in Canada where they could be away from any influence by the "other" parents.

The kids bonded. They played; they swam; they ate ice cream. And they started a new tradition of watching old black and white movies together. It was great.

Then Elizabeth's ex showed up in the same resort town with his new wife and asked to take Erika and Ashley out for ice cream. Elizabeth felt she couldn't say no as the girls, quite young, were excited to go. This caused a lot of resentment for Elizabeth and Keith and the two kids left behind.

Don't be like Elizabeth's ex. Don't intrude.

Traditions Worksheet:

        His   Hers

Easter

_____   _____

Spring Break

_____   _____

Summer Vacation

_____   _____

Thanksgiving

_____   _____

Christmas

_____   _____

Birthdays

_____   _____

Other

_____   _____

Other

_____   _____

Chapter Five: Talk Discipline

Be Consistent

Decide on consistent discipline. Present a united front, but don't discipline your step-children without your spouse present. This is probably one of the most difficult things to do because sometimes your spouse isn't present. But, aside from immediate danger, leave the punishing to the natural parent.

It is far easier to step into the role of disciplinarian if the child is small. Toddlers will be accepting of your authority, but a five year old, a ten year old, and especially a fifteen year old will give you a run for your money. There will be resistance, testing, anger, resentment, and then trouble.

Ease into this role as slowly as possible. Talk over what you already do as far as rewards and punishments, time outs and privileges, etc. If you won't be there for a while, be sure to explain to your child that you've asked their new step-parent to deal out a certain punishment or withdraw a certain privilege if your child steps over the line. Be specific and firm. If the role is reversed and you are in a position to have to discipline your stepchildren, do so in a manner that is free of anger. You can, however, show sympathy and regret on your part.

There will be lots of changes in your new household. You may think that discipline is something that you can back away from now and tackle later. Watch out. It's difficult to get back control if you never had it to begin with. Remember, you're the adult. Think long and hard about this.

Dos and Don'ts

Do be respectful of them.

Do be patient.

Do present a united front.

Don't make too many changes.

Don't take everything personally.

Don't demand their respect. You have to earn it.

Don't be a pushover.

Don't be inconsistent.

Discipline Worksheet:

Write down categories and usual punishments, number of warnings you give, consequences for disobedience, types of acceptable and unacceptable punishments. Discuss these things with your new spouse and be in agreement. The first one is an example:

"Crime"	*# of warnings*	*"Punishment"*
Talking back / Disrespect	_1_	*Apology, loss of screen time*
Hitting / Fighting	—	
Not doing chores	—	
Using foul language	—	
Lying	—	
Aggression or violence	—	
Trouble at school	—	
Coming home late	—	
Cheating	—	
Stealing	—	
	—	
	—	
	—	
	—	

Here are some ideas for consequences:

Loss of TV time

Loss of video games

Loss of computer time

Being grounded

Doing additional chores

Not earning favored activity

Loss of playtime/free time

Loss of cell phone

Losing access to car

And don't forget to have rewards for special behaviors:

Additional phone time

Additional TV time

Additional free time

Additional video game time

Additional computer time

Having someone else do your chore

Gaining additional activity

Staying up later / extending curfew

Chapter Six: Walk the Talk

Dealing with Exes

Never, never, never say anything bad or even slightly negative about your ex or your spouse's ex in front of the kids. Bite your tongue. Bite it now. You will want to slam them, criticize them, and ridicule them. Don't. Not if the kids can hear you.

They already know that you don't get along any more, don't make things worse. Remember, your child derives his or her identity from both of you. Do you want your child to think he or she descended from a moron? They will take it to heart and internalize all the negative stuff.

Try to say only positive things like "your mommy is a good shopper" or "your daddy is very strong." You may think your ex is stubborn, but use a phrase like "he knows how to stick to his guns" instead or else say nothing at all.

You're going to have to talk with your ex about some things, like visitation, holiday plans, school reports, etc., so do so openly, calmly, and civilly.

Your ex may do things like not allow your children to bring

home toys or clothes that he has bought for them. That's a problem between him and your children. Stay out of that argument.

Kiss your children goodbye when they go off with your ex. Avoid saying anything that shows you are sad or hurt that you won't be there too. You don't want your children to feel anxious for you while you're apart or that they shouldn't enjoy their time with the other parent.

If your ex has remarried, too, be extra careful what you say about the new step-parent. Be accepting. You shouldn't want your children to feel they can't love (or even like) this new person because they think you wouldn't approve. That will ruin relationship trust for your children and foster animosities where there shouldn't be any. Let your children love others.

Tell your children the reason you and your ex split up. They can handle it. You may want to say that they'll understand more when they grow up. They will, but don't tell them that now. If you think they're too young to understand, telling them they're too young will only frustrate them and they will begin to invent their own reasons. You don't want that so give them an explanation, a precise but simple one, and that's that. Ask them if they understand. If they do, you're done. Trust me, they'll figure it all out when they grow up.

It will be tempting at times when your child does something negative to compare him or her to your ex. Who hasn't heard a mother say in a disparaging way, "You're just like your father!" or a man say, "You women are all alike"? Remember, your child identifies with both of you. Remarks like this will undermine his or her identification process.

Dos and Don'ts

Don't call your ex names in front of the kids.

Don't play the martyr.

Don't alienate your child from the other parent.

Don't try to buy your kid's love with treats, toys, or privileges that you know your ex wouldn't approve of. Don't be "that" parent.

Don't let your child think he or she had anything to do with you and your ex breaking up.

Don't bash your ex.

Don't belittle your ex's love for your child.

Do speak fairly and in a positive manner about your ex.

True story—names changed:

Angie and Dave successfully managed to get past the ins and outs of their first Christmas together with kids coming and going. They did wonder, however, why they never saw Angie's kids' Christmas presents from her ex.

A little gentle prying revealed that "good old dad" wouldn't let them bring their new things home because he was afraid their step-brother and step-sister might play with and wreck those toys. Angie did the right thing and did not judge her ex-husband's ruling, though she expressed sympathy to her children.

Eventually the kids began sneaking things home in their bags. Angie thought it was sad that they had to deceive their dad.

Worksheet for Dealing with Exes

Write down all the things you cannot say about your ex because it would hurt your child. Do it on another piece of paper and then tear it up and throw it away.

Here are some starters:

I hate _____

It's not fair that _____

Your other parent is _____

Your other parent doesn't _____

My ex treated me like _____ and I think

that _____

I will never tell my child that their other parent

_____

The worst thing about my ex is _____

_____

Chapter Seven: Stop the Talk

When Not to Blend

Don't celebrate your anniversary with your children. Don't expect any recognition of it from them. If you get a card or they say "Happy anniversary" or, miracle of miracles, they throw a party then be very, very happy. To most kids your anniversary (the day your family became blended), though important to you, may not necessarily mark a happy point in the child's life. It may mean the end of their "real" family. It may quite literally be the saddest day of their life though they never told you that.

Your new family may have successfully blended. Step-sisters are best friends. Arguments are few. Family vacations are fun. But still, sorry, they may never acknowledge your anniversary. It may not even be a conscious decision on their part, but subconsciously that day marks a sad point in their lives.

Dos and Don'ts

Do have a happy anniversary.

Don't feel too bad that they ignore it. (Never mind, go ahead and feel bad. We do.)

True story—names changed:

Michelle and Kevin blended two families, raised them with love, handled the usual troubles that kids have while dancing around Michelle's ex's interference and Kevin's first wife's idiosyncrasies.

They saw the kids off to college and later jobs. The kids married; grandchildren came. Twenty five years passed. Michelle and Kevin were excited to have their silver wedding anniversary. They bought a fancy cake, celebrated with the parishioners at their church, and waited to see what their grown children would do.

They did nothing. No acknowledgements were given, no cards were sent, and no gifts arrived, except for a dime store statue that one of the grandchildren presented to them.

Michelle treasures that cheap little statue and keeps it on display, a reminder that her children may never accept the dissolution of their biological parents' marriage and that they will likely never celebrate the step family's success.

Chapter Eight: Family Dynamics

Blended Rules

Treat all the kids equally.

Make sure they know that no one gets more allowance, more presents, or more privileges than anyone else. They are very, very much aware if someone else breaks the rules, gets away with something, gets a special privilege or receives extra attention. I kid you not.

Be sure to make it well known that everyone gets the same treatment and then **give them all the same treatment**.

Set rules early on. Repeat them. Make kids repeat them.

Allow the kids to come up with a rule they'd like others to follow in regards to themselves or their personal possessions. Perhaps they'd like their new step-parent and step-siblings to call them by a particular nickname, or not tease them about something they're sensitive about, or not enter their room without knocking. Listen to *their* rules, discuss them, and follow them as you would expect them to follow the household rules.

Dos and Don'ts

Do create clear rules.

Don't change the rules.

Worksheet for Rules:

Schoolwork (done before TV, phone, dinner?):

_____

_____

Behavior (manners, respect, bullying, courtesy?)

_____

_____

Screen time (sharing computers, video games, surfing?)

_____

_____

Chores (yardwork, bedrooms, laundry, dishwashing, cleaning?)

_____

_____

Miscellaneous (bedtimes, curfews, friends, dating, cars, driving?)

_____

_____

Differences in rules and consequences to discuss with new spouse:

_____

_____

Chapter Nine: Extended Family

Blended Love

Explain really, really carefully to your own parents that they are to think of your step-children as their own grandchildren and to treat them no differently. This is a tough one because it's difficult for a grandparent to suddenly accept someone else's child as their own grandchild. Easier if it's a baby, naturally.

But it's quite sad for a child to grow up loving someone as their grandparent and then being told by that person that he or she isn't really their grandparent. This happened to my children even though that grandfather had been there from the time of their births.

Another example from my own life was when my step-kids heard my mother say she had four grandchildren when by my count she had six: my sister's two, my two, and my two step-children. Though they considered my father to be their grandfather, they could never quite warm up to my mother after that. If you see this happening in your situation please ask your parent to fake it for the sake of those precious kids.

Dos and Don'ts

Do encourage your parents to be accepting.

Don't expect instant love from grandparents.

Chapter Ten: Finances

Money, Money, Money

Work this out with your new spouse before the wedding or soon after. See a lawyer and begin work on a trust, living trust, will, power of attorney, medical advocate forms, etc.

Adjust beneficiaries on life insurances, medical insurances, IRAs, retirement accounts, and pensions.

Decide if you're going to combine checking and savings accounts or keep your individual accounts. List out all of your bills and expenses and decide who's going to pay which bills and expenses.

Don't forget about the kids. Will they get allowances? How much? How often? Are the allowances tied to chores?

Money can be a big problem in some relationships—a power struggle for some or a confusing blind spot for others. Things can quickly go awry if one of you forgets to make the car payment.

Dos and Don'ts

Do put everything in writing

True story—names changed:

Peter and Lily continually had problems with budgeting their money, paying off loans, and managing credit card debt. Lily was better at handling the numbers, but Peter wanted to do this job. He paid some bills by check, used a debit card for other things, and had some items automatically deducted.

Several monthly bills he handled through various apps on his phone including one to make the car payment, but he didn't have a reminder to do it. He forgot one month, then forgot again. His wife, Lily, was working part-time and both of their kids were in school when Lily learned she was pregnant. Peter, clearly distracted by the news, missed another payment.

He was stunned when his car was towed away right out of the parking lot at work. They owed $16,000 on the car. The bank intended to auction off the vehicle, but Lily and Peter would still be liable for the difference.

Fortunately they had a friend who was a bankruptcy lawyer. Unfortunately they had to file for Chapter 13 Bankruptcy in order to protect their assets, mainly their house, and get their car back.

Now Lily takes care of the budget and the bills. Her skills in this regard are better than Peter's. If only they had figured this out sooner.

Worksheet for Budget:

HOUSEHOLD:

Mortgage or rent   _____

Phone   _____

Electricity   _____

Gas   _____

Water and sewer   _____

Cable   _____

Waste removal   _____

Maintenance or repairs   _____

Supplies   _____

Other   _____

TRANSPORTATION:

Vehicle payment   _____

Bus/taxi fare   _____

Insurance   _____

Licensing   _____

Fuel   _____

Maintenance   _____

Other   _____

INSURANCE

Home   _____

Health   _____

Life   _____

Other   _____

FOOD

Groceries   _____

Dining out   _____

Other   _____

PETS

Food   _____

Medical   _____

Grooming   _____

Toys   _____

Other   (Boarding)   _____

PERSONAL CARE

Medical   _____

Hair/nails   _____

Clothing   _____

Dry cleaning   _____

Health club   _____

Organization dues or fees   _____

ENTERTAINMENT

Video/DVD _____

CDs _____

Movies _____

Concerts _____

Sporting events _____

Live theater _____

Other _____

LOANS

Personal _____

Student _____

Credit card _____

Credit card _____

Credit card _____

Other _____

TAXES

Federal _____

State _____

Local _____

Other _____

Total _____

SAVINGS OR INVESTMENTS

Retirement account   _____

Investment account   _____

Other   _____

GIFTS AND DONATIONS

Church   _____

Charity 1   _____

Charity 2   _____

LEGAL

Attorney   _____

Alimony   _____

Payments on lien or judgment_____

Other   _____

TOTAL INCOME   _____

TOTAL EXPENSES   _____

NOTES:

BOOKS by Debra Chapoton

Young adult to Adult:

EDGE OF ESCAPE Innocent adoration escalates to stalking and abduction in this psychological thriller. SOMMERFALLE is the German version of EDGE OF ESCAPE

THE GUARDIAN'S DIARY Jedidiah, a 17-year-old champion skateboarder with a defect he's been hiding all of his life, must risk exposure to rescue a girl that's gone missing.

SHELTERED Ben, a high school junior, has found a unique way to help homeless teens, but he must first bring the group together to fight against supernatural forces.

A SOUL'S KISS When a tragic accident leaves Jessica comatose, her spirit escapes her body. Navigating a supernatural realm is tough, but being half dead has its advantages. Like getting into people's thoughts. Like taking over someone's body. Like experiencing romance on a whole new plane - literally.

EXODIA By 2093 American life is a strange mix of failing technologies, psychic predictions, and radiation induced abilities. Tattoos are mandatory to differentiate two classes, privileged and slave. Dalton Battista fears that his fading tattoo is a deadly omen. He's either the heir of the brutal tyrant of the new capital city, Exodia, or he's its prophesied redeemer.

OUT OF EXODIA In this sequel to EXODIA, Dalton Battista takes on his prophesied identity as Bram O'Shea. When this psychic teen leads a city of 21st century American survivalists out from under an oppressive regime, he puts the escape plan at risk by trusting the mysterious god-like David Ronel.

THE GIRL IN THE TIME MACHINE A desperate teen with a faulty time machine. What could go wrong? 17-year-old Laken is torn between revenge and righting a wrong. SciFi suspense.

THE TIME BENDER A stolen kiss could put the universe at risk. Selina doesn't think Marcum's spaceship is anything more than one heck of a science project … until he takes her to the moon and back.

THE TIME PACER Alex discovered he was half-alien right after he learned how to manipulate time. Now he has to fight the star cannibals, fly a space ship, work on his relationship with Selina, and stay clear of Coreg, full-blooded alien rival and possible galactic traitor. Once they reach their ancestral planet all three are plunged into a society where schooling is more than indoctrination

THE TIME STOPPER Young recruit Marcum learns battle-craft, infiltration and multiple languages at the Interstellar Combat Academy. He and his arch rival Coreg jeopardize their futures by exceeding the space travel limits and flying to Earth in search of a time-bender. They find Selina whose ability to slow the passage of time will be invaluable in fighting other aliens. But Marcum loses his heart to her and when Coreg takes her twenty light years away he remains on Earth in order to develop a far greater talent than time-bending. Now he's ready to return home and get the girl.

THE TIME ENDER Selina Langston is confused about recurring feelings for the wrong guy/alien. She's pretty sure Alex is her soulmate and Coreg should not be trusted at all. But Marcum … well, when he returns to Klaqin and rescues her she begins to see him in a different light.

Non-fiction:

CROSSING THE SCRIPTURES is a Bible Study supplement for anyone who wants to know more about each of the 66 books of the Old and New Testaments.

Children's books:

THE SECRET IN THE HIDDEN CAVE 12-year-old Missy Stark and her new friend Kevin Jackson discover dangerous secrets when they explore the old lodge, the woods, the cemetery, and the dark caves beneath the lake. They must solve the riddles and follow the clues to save the old lodge from destruction.

MYSTERY'S GRAVE After Missy and Kevin solved THE SECRET IN THE HIDDEN CAVE, they thought the rest of the summer at Big Pine Lodge would be normal. But there are plenty of surprises awaiting them in the woods, the caves, the stables, the attic and the cemetery. Two new families arrive and one family isn't human.

BULLIES AND BEARS In their latest adventure at Big Pine Lodge, Missy and Kevin discover more secrets in the caves, the attic, the cemetery and the settlers' ruins. They have to stay one step ahead of four teenage bullies, too, as well as three hungry bears. This summer's escapades become more and more challenging for these two twelve-year-olds. How will they make it through another week?

A TICK IN TIME 12-year-old Tommy MacArthur plunges into another dimension thanks to a magical grandfather clock. Now he must find his way through a strange land, avoid the danger lurking around every corner, and get back home. When he succeeds he dares his new friend Noelle to return with him, but who and what follows them back means more trouble and more adventure.

BIGFOOT DAY, NINJA NIGHT When 12-year-old Anna skips the school fair to explore the woods with Callie, Sydney, Austin, and Natalie, they find evidence of Bigfoot. No way! It looks like his tracks are following them. But that's not the worst part. And neither is stumbling upon Bigfoot's shelter. The worst part is they get separated and now they can't find Callie or the path that leads back to the school.

In the second story Luke and his brother, Nick, go on a boys only camping trip, but things get weird and scary very quickly. Is there a ninja in the woods with them? Mysterious things happen as day turns into night.